T
T
and Heal
While Grieving

Ten Things
To Help You Survive
and Heal
While Grieving

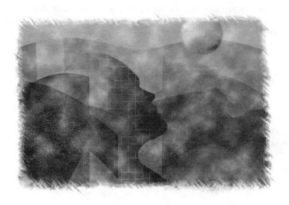

Janet K. Lang

FOREST OF PEACE
Publishing

Suppliers for the Spiritual Pilgrim
Leavenworth, KS

Ten Things to Help You Survive and Heal While Grieving

copyright © 2002, by Janet K. Lang

All rights reserved. No part of this publication may be reproduced or transmitted in any form or by any means, electronic or mechanical, including photocopy, recording, or any information storage or retrieval system, without permission from the publisher.

Library of Congress Cataloging-in-Publication Data

Due to events surrounding September 11, 2001, and subsequent interruptions in U.S. mail delivery and government operations, this data was not yet available at the time of publication. The Cataloging-in-Publication Data for this title may be viewed by searching on the Library of Congress CIP Web site.

published by
Forest of Peace Publishing, Inc.
PO Box 269
Leavenworth, KS 66048-0269   USA
1-800-659-3227
www.forestofpeace.com

printed by
Hall Commercial Printing
Topeka, KS 66608-0007

1st printing: January 2002

To Drew, Chloe and Morgan,
who provide immeasurable joy
and inspiration,
and to Lisa — a true angel

TEN THINGS Contents

Introduction...9

ONE:
Get Professional Help..............................13

TWO:
Keep a Journal..16

THREE:
Make a Contact List.................................20

FOUR:
Set Goals..23

FIVE:
Reach Out to Others for Support............26

SIX:
Have Compassion for Yourself................30

SEVEN:
Talk About Your Grief.............................33

EIGHT:
Pray..36

NINE:
Let Yourself Be Sad..................................39

TEN:
Create New Dreams.................................42

Epilogue...45

You will weep and lament...but your grieving will be turned into joy.
                    —John 16:20

May the God of hope fill you with all joy and peace as you trust in God, so that you may overflow with hope by the power of the Holy Spirit.
                    —Romans 15:13

My period of immense grief began in November of 1999...

I had been sad before — extremely sad, actually, and more than once. But never before had I experienced the paralysis of grief — a kind of pain that literally took my breath away and caused a deep physical, emotional and psychological response that absolutely defied description.

Before my grief began, I was a problem-solver. Rational. Logical. Capable. Feeling and caring, but in control. At least that's how I saw myself. So I was totally unprepared for the "me" I became during a grieving process that lasted nearly two years. I didn't totally fall apart — but my grief became a constant companion. It was like carrying a heavy package, every hour of every day, with no opportunity to rest and put it down for a while.

For me, grieving manifested itself most often with buckets of tears. I would cry so hard and so long that my eyes would swell. This frequently happened at night, and in the morning I would usually wake up feeling slightly better and not quite so hopeless. But then I'd look in the mirror, and my eyelids would still be swollen — a reminder of the hours of crying from the night before. And waves of sadness would again wash over me.

I found that I couldn't wish grief away. Getting angry about being grief-stricken — or about the events that caused my sadness — didn't change a thing. Praying, staying focused, talking — they helped immensely, but the grief was still there. So it came down to the one thing everyone said. The one thing I knew to be true, though I hoped it wasn't: *I had to go through it.* All the things people said about *time healing* were more than just platitudes. I really did have to go through it. I realized that I couldn't change what I was going through and that I had to find the best way to survive it.

Months went by. Although overall I felt I was moving through the grieving process, I was still…what — amazed — shocked — horrified?…to find that I was still crying rivers. Not as often, perhaps. But a lot. Plenty. And almost more than I could bear. But time continued to march on. I continued to *go through it.* Every day, I recommitted myself to surviving this "process" the best way I could.

Nearly two years have gone by since my grieving began. Do I still cry? Absolutely. Buckets? Definitely. But much less often, and with more wisdom. And by now, I have the benefit of all these months that have gone by. I can acknowledge that, yes, good things do come out of bad. I finally believe that I'm going to have a happy life, even though I've experienced sadness that goes beyond anything I could ever begin to put into words.

I can finally say that I survived my grief. I didn't think I'd ever say those words. Though I still get sad, angry and lonely — and still cry more often than I'd like — I can now look back on the past two years and rejoice in the personal growth, deepened spirituality and stronger direction that are the result of my grieving.

This book was not written by a mental health professional or an expert on the stages of grieving. It was written, quite simply, by one who has profoundly experienced grief. Without a doubt, everyone who is grieving has a unique set of circumstances, a personal story and a perspective that cannot be completely understood by anyone else. At the same time, I feel certain that those who know grief also share a great deal. And that is why I wrote this book — in the hope that what helped me might be helpful to someone else.

I doubt that any of these things helped my grief subside more quickly. (I don't think it's possible to speed up the grieving process — and if it *were* possible, I can't imagine it would be healthy.) I do think, though, that these ten things helped me focus and survive life during a time when all I really wanted to do was curl up under a blanket. And I think these things helped me arrive — two years later — at a place in my life that feels *good*. I'm happier, wiser and better directed than I have ever been.

If life is a journey, then a period of grief seems like a very long detour. But I have emerged from it with more love in my heart than I ever thought imaginable. And I see now that grief is not a detour, but an expedition.

The expedition eventually ends.

The journey resumes.

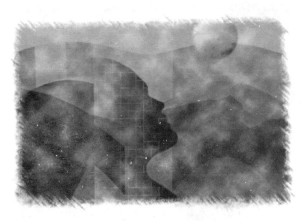

One:
Get Professional Help

Lots of people see a therapist, and many visit a psychiatrist. I believe that seeking help is a sign of strength…and I saw both. Often. And I poured my heart out to them. They helped me immeasurably, providing me with anti-depressants to help me through the endless sadness and emotional support for my trauma and grief.

I had to visit a few therapists and a few psychiatrists before I found the ones with whom I "clicked." Some that I visited were probably very nice people, but I sure didn't enjoy talking with them. One psychiatrist I met with asked me a series of questions while taking notes, never looked at my face, handed me a prescription, and had me out the door in about three minutes. *HEY! I'm grieving here!* I wanted to say. I'm glad I kept searching, because the next doctor I visited was warm and compassionate, and truly wanted to know about my grief, the cause, and how I was coping. He was encouraging, honest and validating.

I quickly found a therapist whom I loved. I looked forward to my appointment with her every week…and sometimes, when things were really bad for me, twice a week. But three months into our sessions together, she told me that she was moving out of the state in three weeks. I was traumatized and sat there in total disbelief. I had no idea what I would do without her emotional support. She felt awful about it, too, and almost started crying while I sat there bawling.

In the midst of this added trauma, it occurred to me that I had to do something. I could be angry and feel betrayed and wallow in my additional sorrow — or I could find a new therapist. Something amazing even crossed my mind. *Maybe*, I thought, *I'll find someone that will help me even more than this person already has.*

Well, guess what. That's exactly what happened. I made appointments with two therapists who were recommended to me. The first one was AWFUL (at least, to me). I left there feeling horrible, sad and frustrated. But the next week, I visited LeeAnn. From the first minute we spoke, she seemed to see the big picture that was my life. We *connected*. And LeeAnn has proven to be an incredible blessing in my life. She has given me insight into my life, my situation, my grief and my healing journey. With her encouragement and skill, I have discovered many important things about myself that have given additional meaning to my life.

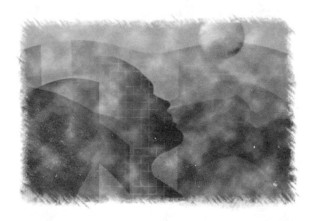

Two: Keep a Journal

Most every therapist tells you to keep a journal. Every time I'd hear that suggestion I'd think, "I write all day! That's what I do for a living! The last thing I want to do is add to that by spending time writing down what I'm feeling." I was very stubborn about it and thought that maybe some people needed to journal, but not me. But one night, all of a sudden, I started to do it. And surprise, surprise. It really did help.

It's amazing what I discovered about what I was feeling when I wrote in my journal. I think that writing — especially free-flowing writing that is meant for one's own eyes only — opens up windows in the heart and soul that otherwise may remain locked shut.

Most of the time, I'd write in my journal when I was in the depths of my despair. I'd write down thoughts that were so sad, they were really tragic. It's how I was feeling at that moment, and it was important to get it down on paper. Later on, during moments when my spirits were somewhat lifted, I'd read what I had written and realize that I didn't always feel *quite* that gloomy.

At one point, I got tired of doing a traditional journal. So I bought a small spiral-bound book full of thick pages. And I bought a box of colorful markers. I wrote "Janet's Book of Thoughts" on the cover of the book and began keeping a completely different kind of journal.

In this journal, I'd let my creativity take over in expressing what was on my mind. I'd write a five-word sentence (*I AM TIRED OF CRYING!*) over and over in big, bold letters. I doodled on the borders, and drew broken hearts, sad faces and big teardrops.

Every once in a while, I'd find a magazine article that was somehow meaningful to me. I'd tear it out and paste it into my thought book. Pictures went in there, too. Anything I wanted — it was *mine* and *mine only.*

Here's the most important thing I found about keeping a journal: It helps you see how far you've come. About six months after I started it, when I read everything I wrote the first month, I thought, *Whew! I know I'm sad now, and I know I was sad then, but I didn't realize how much sadder I was then than I am now.* I think this was an important revelation, since the grieving process isn't linear. You don't start off sad on GRIEF DAY ONE and feel a little less sad every day until one day you wake up and the grief is GONE. No — it's more of a two steps forward, one step back kind of thing. So it's difficult to keep track of your progress, and that's why journaling your thoughts can really help.

A friend told me about something she did in her journal during a long period of grief. Each time she wrote in her journal, she rated herself emotionally on a scale of 1 to 10, with "1" being extremely sad and "10" being extremely happy — and noted that on her journal entry. She said that for the first six months, the numbers were usually 1 or 2, with an occasional 3. For the second six months, the numbers were usually 3, 4 or 5.

As time went on, she continued to move up the scale. The most valuable part of doing this, she said, was seeing during that second six months she really had made progress. "I still felt so sad," she said, "but I realized I wasn't nearly as sad as I *had been*. That helped me have hope for the future."

THREE:
Make a Contact List

When I was at my lowest, early in the grieving process, there were times when I would be so distraught that I truly could not think of what to do. My emotional pain was so deep during these spells, and I would cry so hard, that I had no idea what or who could help me, what I should do or where to turn. The depth of my despair was, to be honest, very frightening. And since these painful times often came late at night, I was even less aware of what to do or whom I could turn to for support.

Following one of those painful evenings, it occurred to me that I should be prepared for those times when my sadness would completely take over every ounce of my being. So while I was feeling somewhat okay and thinking clearly, I made a list of people I could call, if I needed to, when my heart was truly in splinters. I literally thought about every single person on the planet that I know, and I created a list of those I knew I could call at any time while crying hysterically or depressed beyond words. My list included people who knew me well, and some who weren't close friends but that I knew cared and were compassionate and good listeners. Then I went back and marked an "A" or "B" by each name, thus establishing a hierarchy of who would truly be the most helpful when I was at my emotional bottom.

I used the list many times. It's amazing how clearly I could think of these friends and family members when I was feeling okay … but how clouded my thinking was in that regard when I was in my most grief-stricken state.

As time went on, I altered my list. There were names on the original list that were scratched off, if I found out that they were not able to provide the emotional support I needed. (Some people are great people but aren't at their best when someone is sobbing on the other end of the phone.) And as I developed some new relationships and friendships, names were added. I didn't make a call *every single time* I cried — but for those times when I felt totally isolated and beyond hope, a call to a supportive person made a huge difference.

Four:
Set Goals

About six weeks into my grieving process, I felt absolutely paralyzed. I was a single mother, and self-employed...so I couldn't exactly spend every day in bed or staring out the window (which is what I wanted to do). I started thinking about what I could do to bring any element of joy or satisfaction to my life — and immediately felt overwhelmed by doing those things. But one afternoon, during a few hours when my mood felt somewhat elevated, I decided to think longer-term. I defined some goals for myself based on things that I felt would make my life richer and more fulfilling.

These goals were set by category: personal, social, family, parenting spiritual and professional. Then, since it happened to be early January at the time, I established specific goals for myself based on each quarter of the year. Here are a few excerpts from that list.

Personal:

First quarter
Exercise 15 minutes every day

Second quarter
Do an art project

Social:

First quarter
Call a friend every day

Second quarter
Schedule lunch or dinner with a friend once a month

Parenting:

First quarter
Take kids out for dinner once a week

Second quarter
Plan a weekend away with the kids

Family:

First quarter
E-mail or call parents and sister at least once a week

Second quarter
Schedule a visit to parents

Spiritual:

First quarter
Find a new church

Second quarter
Read one book with a spiritual theme

Professional:

First quarter
Attend two networking events each month

Second quarter
Create new marketing materials for company

I typed up these goals, printed them out and put them in a private place in my planner. I reviewed them often…and they helped me *a lot.* Having these goals in writing helped me focus on what I needed to do during those many, many sad days when I really had no idea *what* to do.

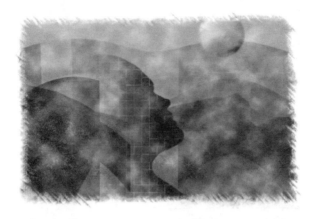

Five:
Reach Out to Others for Support

One of my first-quarter goals under the "spiritual" category was to find a new church. I did so fairly quickly, and found it offered many programs, classes and services that provided support in times of need.

Should I call about some of these programs at the church? I wondered. *No one knows me there. I haven't even joined yet. I don't know what to do.* I thought about it for a few weeks. And then, one day during a church service I noticed an article in the bulletin about the church's Stephen Minister program. This program provided specially trained lay ministers to any church member or visitor in need of emotional support. There was a form enclosed to request a Stephen Minister...and before I could talk myself out of it, I filled out the form and dropped it in the offering plate.

Within a week, I received a call from the program's coordinator. She was kind, caring and respectful. She didn't ask why I needed a Stephen Minister or request any information or details about my life. Her job was to find out when I was available to meet, get a feel for my personality, then pray about the best person to assign to me. Within another week, I got a call from Patsy — my Stephen Minster. We had a pleasant conversation and set up a time to get together the following week.

Five minutes after Patsy and I met, I knew she was someone who would make a difference in my life. She was a wonderful listener and supported me as I grieved. She encouraged me, but at the same time allowed me to be sad. I could call her any time, and she truly became an important support person in my life.

Once I started being less sad and more happy, Patsy and I agreed that we should end our Stephen Minister relationship. But I'm glad to say that by that time, a wonderful friendship had developed. She's still there for me — and now, I'm there for her, too. Patsy never would have become an important person in my life if I hadn't reached out for help.

I also met with several of the pastors one-on-one at my church to ask advice and seek spiritual guidance. Their compassion during the height of my grieving process was just what I had hoped it would be.

I realize now that it's important, while grieving, to have the support of people who tell you, "It's okay that you're sad. Don't rush it. Go ahead and just be as sad as you need to be." Sometimes, the people who know you and love you the most aren't going to say that — because your being sad is just too painful for *them*. They'd rather you act a little happier and get through it a little sooner. So meeting with a pastor was an important way for me to just put my grief and sadness and turmoil right out there and hear someone say, "Let me pray for you. Let me hold your hand and be there for you in your sadness."

Anyway, the bottom line is this: I realized that I needed help, support and a lot of caring people in my life…and I knew that to get that, I had to reach out. No one could read my mind and know what I needed. *I had to reach out. And it made a big difference.*

Six:
Have Compassion for Yourself

I have to admit, it's LeeAnn who first told me about this one.

During one of my therapy sessions I was talking about, as usual, my intense sadness and how tired I was of thinking about being sad and feeling sad and just living a sad life. To LeeAnn, I guess it sounded like I was criticizing myself for how I was feeling. She said to me, "Janet, you're a caring and compassionate person. If someone you know had something awful happen in their life, wouldn't you say to them, 'I'm sorry you're so sad. I don't blame you for feeling sad. If that had happened to me, I would feel sad too.'"

Yes, I said. *I would say those things.*

Well, LeeAnn told me in no uncertain terms that I had to be just as compassionate with myself as I was with other people. That was quite a revelation for me! Offer myself compassion? You mean…*feel sorry for myself?*

Then I realized something. I had every reason to feel sorry for myself. I mean, something had happened in my life that had given me unspeakable pain and sorrow. OF COURSE I should feel sorry for myself!

Feeling sorry for myself didn't mean giving up on working through my grief. It didn't mean I had to tell anyone that I was offering compassion to myself or that I said to myself over and over, *I feel sorry for me.* It was just an important frame of mind to have as I survived each day.

I've been through something awful, I'd think. *It's understandable that I feel so extremely sad. Anyone would feel sad in this situation. I have good reason to cry so much.*

And I will give myself the time I need to heal. Offering compassion to myself proved to be an important part of my healing.

Being compassionate with myself allowed me fully to *feel* my pain rather than pushing it away or keeping it at arm's length. It allowed me to go gradually through my pain rather than around it.

Seven:
Talk About Your Grief

I'm sure there are people in my life who have heard me say "I'm so sad" about a million times. But if they're tired of it — they never let on. And that was a tremendous help to me.

Of course, the majority of people in my life — business associates, casual acquaintances, etc., had no idea that I was grieving during all of those months. But there were a handful of people (not counting my therapist and psychiatrist) who knew how sad I was and were kind and caring and willing to listen during all those months as I grieved.

I felt like a broken record, but I just needed to talk about my grief to help me survive. I talked about what had happened that led to my sadness, and I talked about my sadness itself. I talked about how lonely, scared and isolated I felt. I talked about how all my hopes for the future had faded. I talked about how tired I was of feeling everything I was feeling.

My neighbor, Anita, was one of the people at the top of my contact list. She knew about everything that had happened and why I was so very, very sad. There were times when I just couldn't bear to be alone with my grief, and I would knock on her door or give her a call. She would sit with me and hug me and I would cry. And talk. And cry. Early on, especially, I sometimes wondered what I would have done without Anita so close by.

I'm a big believer in support groups, and I searched for one I could join. I had trouble finding one that seemed to fit my situation, and those I did identify met at times that logistically were just not possible for me. Although I survived my grief expedition without participating in a support group, I truly believe it would have been an added help.

Talking is a huge part of healing. There are some people in the world who may be wonderful in other ways but aren't at their best when it comes to listening to people talk about their sadness. I knew the people in my life who were *great* at listening and providing support — and I talked to them about my sadness…over and over and over.

EIGHT:
Pray

My spirituality was blossoming in the months before my long period of grief began. But after I was thrown into mind-numbing sadness, I found myself praying *a lot*. I didn't know very much about God, but I knew I needed strength anywhere I could find it — and from what I had heard, God was one definite source.

Prayer worked for me. I had long, tearful conversations with God. I asked God why this had happened to me. Why I was in this situation. When I was going to stop hurting.

How long I was going to cry every day. But most of all, I asked God for exactly what I needed: strength. I asked God to give me the strength to make it through every day. The strength to come out of my grief a better, stronger person. The strength to see a way to use all of that pain in a positive way.

God gave me the strength that I prayed for. Through prayer, I found myself looking at my grief in a larger context. I became more aware of the way God was working in my life. And I saw that although God didn't want me to suffer, He did want me to grow in my love for Him and everyone here on earth as the result of my pain.

It's hard to say what my relationship with God would be like had I not gone through such a lengthy period of grief. But I do know that as a result of what I've been through, I know the wonder of God and the amazing power He has to turn bad into good if we will allow Him to do His work. I thank God every day for giving me a resilient spirit and for allowing me to come out of such a sad, sad time in my life with a soaring spirit.

LeeAnn pointed something out to me once that helped me see why grief is so important. She said, "God made us with memories. He could have made us so that we'd go through something profoundly painful, and two days later forget all about it. But He didn't do that. He made us with memories, so that we would feel pain and then remember what caused it. But He also made us capable of learning from that pain and using what we have learned to make our lives even better." It is through the wonder of God that I am where I am today.

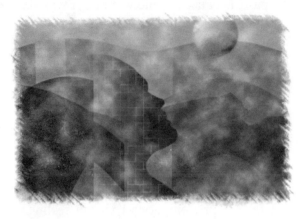

Nine:
Let Yourself Be Sad

There are times in life, let's face it, when you can't show just how sad you really are. I couldn't cry in front of my clients, for example. And I managed to hold it together when I was meeting with my kids' teachers or other people I didn't know very well.

But one thing I didn't do — especially during those early months when my grief was most intense — was put on a happy face for everyone. This doesn't mean that I was a total sad sack every hour of every day when I was with people who knew me well. That's not the case. Because as time went on, I was able to function okay and felt…well, not happy, but just sort of so-so.

When I was really sad, though, I let myself be really sad. I never imagined I could let so many people see me cry and not feel totally embarrassed about it. My "normal" (pre-grief) personality was always very upbeat…but it wasn't important to me that I be *that person* while going through such sadness. I did not put on a happy face. I did not fake happy emotions I wasn't feeling. I did not feel obligated to act cheerful just to make people around me feel better. I just let me be me.

Letting myself be sad extended to the times when I was alone too. When I felt overwhelmed with sadness, I completely allowed myself to cry. There was no reason to try and talk myself out of the tears or attempt to distract myself with work or anything else. I figured that if I was going to cry, it might as well be a *really good cry.* And after months of those really good cries, I began to see how cleansing they were. There were even hints that following a long, hard cry I perhaps moved a teeny bit along the grief continuum — that those tears were a vital part of the healing process.

So I let myself truly feel sadness. I looked at pictures and listened to music that triggered even more tears. Even now it's hard to believe these words, but it's true: *Allowing myself to become immersed in sadness always led to my feeling a little less sad.*

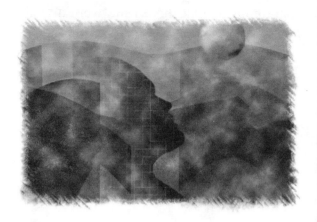

Ten:
Create New Dreams

After many, many months of just feeling *SAD*…it began to dawn on me that perhaps I could create new dreams for myself. At one point in my life — not so long ago — I had so many dreams. But while I grieved and cried and mourned, those dreams seemed to wash away. Many months had to go by before I realized that I could come up with new dreams.

One way I did this was to rediscover myself. I know it sounds almost contradictory to suggest that I did this while I was grieving, but in many ways it's true. And I think I know why.

When I was feeling sad, I often felt that I couldn't go on. There were many days that I didn't *want* to go on. It wasn't that I didn't feel there was anything worth living for — it's just that my emotional pain was so intense that I almost couldn't take it at times.

So eventually, to go on with my life, I decided to do something different — to find new reasons to get up every day. I wanted to make myself feel special and tap into talents and God-given gifts that had long ago been set aside. I had a strong will to awaken my spirit and give my wilted heart a jump start.

It was when I reached this point — near the end of my grieving process — that new dreams began to take shape. I realized that my life could take many directions — and I didn't have to follow the same path I'd been on before the grieving began. There were many things about me and within me that had been hidden from the world for many years — even hidden from myself. But as I emerged from a painful fog that lasted nearly two years, things began to be much clearer. New gifts, inner resources and a sense of direction came to light as a result of the grieving process. Another one of God's miracles? Of course. But what I did with this rediscovery was totally up to me.

With my renewed energy for life, I've created new dreams for myself. I see now that without dreams — without hope — sadness persists. I'm a little more realistic with these dreams — because once you've encountered true grief, it's impossible to deny that things don't always go as planned. But my grief expedition has come to an end. My new hopes and dreams have placed me solidly back into my journey of life.

God comforts us in all our troubles, so that we can comfort those in any trouble with the comfort we ourselves have received from God.

—2 Corinthians 1:4

Epilogue

While writing this book, words poured forth from my heart that made clear the pain and sadness I felt during a two-year process of grieving. And now, I am living proof that one does survive grief. I am still journaling and seeing a therapist. I reach out to my friends, set goals for myself, and know those I can call on to help me through a difficult day. When

I feel sad, I let myself be sad. I continue to assure myself that my grief was well founded — and I talk about it with people in my life who understand that I still have some healing to do. I pray — more than ever. And I focus on the new dreams I have created for my life — dreams that are beginning to come true and are nothing short of miracles when I think back to the hopelessness I felt in November of 1999.

Has my experience with grief changed me? Definitely — and in ways that are fulfilling and worthy of celebration. I now have tremendous compassion for others who are hurting — compassion beyond what I ever could have imagined feeling. I will now hug a stranger who is crying. I will now pray for someone I meet who seems lost or has a faraway look. I will not judge a person whose behavior seems out-of-character, inappropriate or difficult. After all, I know it's possible that anyone I encounter may be grieving — and those who are grieving must have love, reassurance, understanding and warmth. I received it while I was going through grief, and now I seek opportunities to provide that support to others.

This, I believe, is the part of grieving that truly demonstrates the beauty of God's plan for those of us on earth. And I believe with all my heart that when we emerge from a period of grief we are strengthened and fortified by God — and in turn, we can offer hope, encouragement and love to others walking a painful path. It is one of God's greatest desires that we share our gifts with others — and you can be certain that one day, someone in pain will be healed because of the grief that is now your constant companion. One day, your experience with grief will become an invaluable gift. Please don't lose faith while you wait for that day to arrive.